around india in 26 alphabets

KARISHMA MIRPURI

Illustrated by Maethawee Chiraphong

ISBN: 978-2-211-80510-0

Printed in Bangkok, Thailand

UNITED LASTING GROUP

Dedication Page

To my husband and children, without whom this book would have been completed a long time ago. Thank you all for being my excuse for procrastinating.

To my Hindi/Sindhi-speaking parents and NS family, thank you for never teaching me Hindi so that I could create this book to teach my children the basics.

To my million brothers, sisters, uncles, aunties, and nieces and nephews whom I have sent this to a thousand times before it got published - Shukriya!
I love you all

To you the reader, I hope you ENJWAYYYY!
P.s. I also love you

ANAAR
AAKASH
AUNTIES
ANDA
ALOO
Aa

BOLLYWOOD
BILLEE
BANDAR
BABA
BHUTTA
BAKRI
Bb

CHUMMA
CHAAT CORNER
CHAIWALA
CHAAND
CHANDNI CHOWK
चांदनी चौक
CHOR
CHOOHA
CRICKET
Cc

DIWALI
DEVI
DUKAAN
DISHOOM
DULHAN
DOODH
Dd

EENT
ELAICHI
EID
EKTARA
EK
ੴ
Ee

FOOGA
FILUM
CINEMA
Falooda
FATNA
Ff
FAKIR

GAADEE
GOBAR
GAUR
GHODA
GHEE
GULAB
Gg

HORN
OK
PLEASE
HAATHEE
HOLI
HARA
HANUMAN
Hh
HAATH

INDRADHANUSH
INDIA GATE
IMAARAT
INDRA GANDHI INTL. AIRPORT
Ii
IMLI

JHANDA
Jaipur
JOOTE
Jalebi
30
JAAN
JODHPURI
I INDIA
Jj
JAADOO

KUMBH MELA
KITAB
KABADDI
KUTTA
KATHAK
Kk

LADAKH
LOMRI
LATTOO
LAHASUN
LUNGHI
Ll

MURGHEE
MACHALEE
MATKA
MEHNDI
MOTORSAIKIL
Mm

NO SPITTING
NARIYAL
NANI
NAHIN
Nn
NAMASTE
NAAV

Odisha
OONT
OKHLI
OCI
OHM
OONGALEE
Oo

PUNE
PATANG
PANI PURI
PANDIT
Pp
PANI
PAAN

Qq
QUTAB MINAR
QILA
!?
QALAM

REL GAADEE
RICKSHAW
RUPEES
RAKHI
ROTI
Rr

SANGEET
SITAR
SOOAR
SARI
SAMOSA
Ss
shaadi.com

TAJ MAHAL
TOPEE
TAULIYA
THALI
Tt
TIFFIN

ULLOO
UDGHOSH
ULTI
ULJHAN
UPHAAR
Uu

VAASTU
VARNAMALA
VIR
VAADA
VADA
Vv

DHOBI WALA
WAQT
WAGHOLI
TIFFIN WALA
MITHAI WALA
Ww

XEROX
XELDEM, GOA
XCUUJ ME
XEROX
XEROX
X-RAY
Xx

YAATRI
YOGI
YAMUNA
YAAR
YOGA
Yy

13
ZEBRA
ZEE TV
ZABARDAST
KNOCK
KNOC
ZUKHAM
ZAMEENDAR
Zz

Glossary

A

Aam - mango
Aloo - potato
Anaar - pomegranate
Aunties
Angoor - grapes
Aakash - sky
Arranged Marriage
Adrak - ginger
Amrood - guava

B

Bollywood
Buddha
Bhutta - corn
Bandar - monkey
BIlli - cat
Bakri - goat
Baccha - child
Bijilee - electricity wires
Bhaaloo - bear
Bhojan - meal
Biryani - famous rice dish
Baba - holy man
Bhindi - okra
Banyan Tree
Baaltee - pail

C

Chumma - kiss
Cricket
Chidiya - bird
Chaand - moon
Chooha - mouse
Chandni Chowk - shopping district in Delhi
Chashma - glasses
Chai - tea
Chaat - means "to lick" but is also a popular street food
Chappal - slippers
Chor - thief
Chachi - aunt
Chole - chick peas
Carom board - popular board game
Choodiyan - bangles
Chipkali - lizard

D

Diwali - festival of lights
Dulhan - bride
Dosa - crepe/thin pancake
Doodh - milk
Dishoom - popular sound of gunshots in old Indian movies
Dukaan - a shop
Dholak/ Dhol - two headed drum
Dandiya - stick dance of Gujarati origin
Diya - candle
Dibba - box
Darwaja/darwaza - door
Delhi - India Gate

E

Elaichi - cardamom
Eent - brick

Ek - one
Easter eggs
Ektara - stringed instrument

F

Filum - movie
Fatna - burst - ie a burst tyre
Fattaphat - going fast
Firangi - foreigner
Falooda - ice cream desert made with sabja seeds
Fooga - balloon
Fakir - ascetic usually of Muslim origin

G

Gaadee - car
Gobar - cow dung
Gulaab - color pink
Gulaab gang
Ganges - famous river in India
Ghee - clarified butter
Ganesh - Hindu Elephant God - remover of obstacles
Gulab jamun - sweet round brown dessert
Gaur - ox
Ghoda - horse
Ghar - home
Gadha - donkey
Gophan - sling

H

Holi - festival of colors
Hanuman - Monkey God
Hara - green color
Hathee - elephant
Horn OK Please - famous saying on trucks
Hijra - tranny
Haar - necklace
Haath - hand
Haldi - turmeric (yelllow color in the picture)
Hathauda - hammer

I

Indradhanush - rainbow
Indra Gandhi airport
India gate
Imli - tamarind
Ik Baal - loosely translates to "one hair"
Imaarat - buildings

J

Jaan - lovers
Jaipur
Jhulelal - Sindhi God
Juice corner
Jalebi - deep fried sweet dessert soaked in syrup
Joda - a pair
Jodhpuris - formal mens suits
Joote - shoes
Jaadoogar - magician
Jhanda - flag

K

Kulfi - traditional ice cream
Krishna - God who is 8th avatar of Lord Vishnu
Kitaab - book
Kainchee - scissors
Kali - known as the Black Goddess
Kela - banana
Kathak - Indian classical dance

Kamal - lotus flower
Kabootar - pigeon
Kaka - informally used for poop
Kabaddi - contact team sport
Kutta - dog
Kumbh mela - pilgrimage festival

L

Ladakh
Lungi - mens sarong
Lehsun - garlic
Lattoo - spinning top
Lomri - fox
Lauki - veggie
Lota - vessel
Ladaka - boy
Ladaki - girl
Lakdi - wood
Lifaafa - envelope
Lengha - ankle length traditional skirt

M

Mataka - pot
Motorsaikil - motorcycle
Machhlee - fish
Murgi - chicken
Mojari - shoes
Mehendi - body art paste made from henna leaves
Moonh - mouth
Monsoon
Mandap - covering
Mor - peacock
Matches - Maachis
Mirchi - chili
Moonchh - moustache
Masala - spices

N

Nimbu - lemon
Nahin - no
Naga - snake
Namaste - salutation
Nani - maternal grandma
Nariyal - coconut
Nanha baccha - small child
Nazar - evil eye
Nirma - washing powder
Naav - boat
Neela - blue
Nose - naak
Naach - dance

O

Odisha
OCI - Overseas Citizenship of India booklet
Octopus
Oont - camel
Om - sacred sound of the Universe used as a mantra
Okay
Oongalee - finger
Okhli - mortar/pounder

P

Pune
Pride parade - LGBTQIA community celebrations
Pani Puri - famous street food made of a puffed wheat ball filled with potatoes and flavored water
Pani - water
Paan - betel leaf

Paisa - 1/100 of a Rupee
Pandit - scholar of Hinduism
Peela - yellow
Phool - flowers
Popat - butterfly
Patang - kite
Pulis - police
Pagadee - turban
Papeeta - papaya
Patte - playing cards

Q

Qutab Minar - monument in New Delhi
Qila - fort
Qalam - fountain pen
Q - Kyu? - why?

R

Roti - flatbread
Rasmalai - dessert made of cottage cheese balls **soaked** in sweet milk
Rasam - spicy South Indian soup served as a side
Rupee - currency of India
Raja - king
Rani - queen
Rel gaadee - train
Rickshaw - 3 wheeler vehicle
Rangoli - art form meaning rows of colors
Rassee - rope
Rakhi - thread or talisman sisters tie to brothers on Raksha Bandhan
Rona - crying

S

Sangeet - Indian celebration part of a wedding function - translates to “musical night”
Surya - sun
Sitaare - stars
Shankh - conch
Samosa - pastry with savory filling
Sari - traditional draped dress
Sardar - people of Sikh community
Sita - Goddess Sita
Sitar - stringed instrument
Sri Ram - Lord Ram
Sadhu - religious ascetic
Sitaphaal - custard apple
Skootar - scooter
Sooar - pig
Sher - lion
Seb - apple
Sharaab - alcohol

T

Tauliya - towers
Topee - hat
Tandoori - food cooked in a “tandoor” oven
Tamaatar - tomato
Thali - plate usually filled with different kinds of foods
Tarbooz - watermelon
Tel - oil
Thaila - bag
Tota - parrot
Tilak - colored mark worn on forehead - can be red/yellow/white
Tiffin box - set of food containers
Takla- bald

U

Ulloo - owl
Upma - dish usually made from semolina
Uppam - type of food
Utsav - celebration
Uppar - up

V

Vishnu - Lord Vishnu the pervader
Varsha - rain
Vimaan - airplane
Vidyalay - school
Vir - brave
Vijay - winner
Vastragar - wardrobe

W

Wala - masculine form used to describe someone's profession
Wali - feminine form used to describe someone's profession
Chai wala - the one with tea
Tiffin wala - the one who sends food to people
Dhobi wala - the one who washes clothes
Rickshaw wala - rickshaw driver
Sari wali - sari seller
Mithai wala - sweets seller
Phanka wala - someone who fans fans
Waqt - time
Doodh wala - milk seller
Karne wala - worker

Xerox
X-ray
Excuuj me please
Xeldem - place in Goa

Yoga - spiritual discipline
Yogi - one who practices yoga
Yamuna river
Yaadein - memories
Yaar - friends

Z

Zindagi - life
Zabardast - force
Zamindar - landlord/land owner
Zebra
Zukham - sick

www.ingramcontent.com/pod-product-compliance
Lightning Source LLC
LaVergne TN
LVHW071135300726
844417LV00028BA/87